A Day in Mexico

Cynthia Rosenthal

Infomax Readers

Rosen Classroom™

New York

Published in 2014 by The Rosen Publishing Group, Inc.
29 East 21st Street, New York, NY 10010

Book Design: Jon D'Rozario

Photo Credits: Cover, p. 5 Golden Pixels LLC/Shutterstock.com; p. 7 Gallo Gallina/The Bridgeman Art Library/Getty Images; p. 9 (frame) Pixel Embargo/Shutterstock.com; p. 9 (mountains) Anton_Ivanov/Shutterstock.com; p. 9 (beach) holbox/Shutterstock.com; p. 9 (forest) ecco3d/Shutterstock.com; pp. 9, 22 (background) Magone/Shutterstock.com; p. 11 (airplane) MO_SES/Shutterstock.com; p. 11 (map) Volina/Shutterstock.com; p. 13 Andy Dean Photography/Shutterstock.com; p. 15 Nayashkova Olga/Shutterstock.com; p. 17 Al Bello/Getty Images Sport/Getty Images; p. 19 CHRISTIAN DE ARAUJO/Shutterstock.com; p. 21 Frontpage/Shutterstock.com.

ISBN: 978-1-4777-2315-9
6-pack ISBN: 978-1-4777-2316-6

Manufactured in the United States of America

CPSIA Compliance Information: Batch #CS13RC: For further information contact Rosen Publishing, New York, New York at 1-800-237-9932.

Contents

A Family Trip!

Gabriella is going on a trip to Mexico. She'll get to visit her cousin Luis. He lives in Mexico with Gabriella's Aunt Rosa and Uncle Miguel. Gabriella's parents were born in Mexico, too. Then, they moved to the United States.

Gabriella has never been to another country before! She can't wait to see for herself what a day is like where Luis lives.

Gabriella's parents moved from Mexico to the United States to start a new life for themselves before she was born.

Learning About Mexico

Gabriella wants to learn as much as she can about Mexico before her trip. She asks her mom to tell her about Mexican history. Gabriella's mom tells her about the native people who lived in the area we now call Mexico for thousands of years. Then, Spanish **explorers** crossed the ocean and ruled the people there. Mexico became a free country in 1821.

The Spanish explorers fought the native people for control of the land in Mexico.

Gabriella also wants to know what Mexico looks like. Her dad shows her pictures he took of different places in Mexico before he left to live in America.

Gabriella sees pictures of beaches and **tropical** forests. She also sees a picture of tall mountains. Her dad says these are the Sierra Madre (see-EHR-uh MAH-dray). Mexico has many mountains!

If you visit Mexico, you can see these beautiful places for yourself!

Capital Cities

Gabriella and her family live just outside of Washington, DC. This is the capital of the United States. Luis and his family live in the capital of Mexico, which is Mexico City. More people live in Mexico City than in any other city in Mexico.

Gabriella and her parents take an airplane to go to Mexico City. It's her first airplane trip!

It takes about four hours to fly from Washington, DC, to Mexico City.

UNITED STATES
Washington, DC
MEXICO
Mexico City

Meeting Luis

Gabriella's day with Luis begins when she meets him at the airport in Mexico City. He gives her a big hug and says hello to her in both English and Spanish. Spanish is the main language spoken in Mexico, just as English is the main language spoken in the United States. Luis learns English at school and practices it by himself at home.

Gabriella learned how to say "cousin" in Spanish all by herself. It's *primo*!

So Much Food!

After Gabriella's family leaves the airport, it's time to eat lunch. In Mexico, this is the biggest meal of the day. Aunt Rosa cooks it all by herself. She makes rice, chicken, and a kind of flat bread made with corn. This is called a tortilla (tohr-TEE-yuh).

For dessert, Gabriella eats flan. It's made with eggs, milk, sugar, and vanilla.

Gabriella loves all the food her Aunt Rosa cooks for her family!

Playing Soccer

Gabriella goes with Luis to play with his friends. He loves to play sports with his friends after school and on weekends. Gabriella likes to play sports, too! Her **favorite** sport is baseball.

Luis's favorite sport is soccer. In Mexico, soccer is called *fútbol*. It's the most **popular** sport in the whole country! Gabriella plays on her school's soccer team, so she likes playing with Luis and his friends.

Luis and his friends like to play soccer every day!

Music and Dancing

At night, Gabriella and her family go to see a special kind of Mexican band play in the city. It's called a mariachi (mahr-ee-AH-chee) band. The band plays **traditional** Mexican music. Gabriella and her family see special Mexican dancers, too.

Gabriella buys treats for herself and her friends back home. She uses money she saved for the trip. In Mexico, the money they use is called the peso (PAY-soh).

The people in the mariachi band and the Mexican dancers wear traditional Mexican clothes. Gabriella thinks they look really cool!

A Great Day!

Gabriella had fun during her day with Luis. She learned a lot about where her family came from and where some of them still live. Her favorite part of her trip was finally meeting her cousin! Gabriella liked seeing how different his life at home is from her life.

Gabriella didn't want to say goodbye to Luis, but there were other places in Mexico for her to see. She saw lots of cool places during her trip!

Gabriella wants to travel to Mexico by herself when she grows up!

Two Different Lives

Gabriella and Luis live in two very different countries. These are just some of the ways Gabriella's life is different from Luis's life.

	Gabriella (United States)	Luis (Mexico)
capital	Washington, DC	Mexico City
language	English	Spanish
favorite sport	baseball	fútbol
biggest meal	dinner	lunch
money	dollar	peso

Glossary

explorer (ihk-SPLOHR-uhr) Someone who travels to find new places.

favorite (FAY-vuh-ruht) Liked best.

popular (PAH-pyuh-luhr) Well liked.

traditional (truh-DIH-shuh-nuhl) Handed down within a group of people for many years.

tropical (TRAH-pih-kuhl) Having to do with an area of the world known for warm and wet weather.

Index